IN THIS ISSUE:

tourism.com TATTLER
ISSUE 08 AUGUST 2016

PUBLISHER
Tourism Tattler (Pty) Ltd.
PO Box 891, Umhlanga Rocks, 4320
KwaZulu-Natal, South Africa.
Website: www.tourismtattler.com

EXECUTIVE EDITOR Des Langkilde
Cell: +27 (0)82 374 7260
Fax: +27 (0)86 651 8080
E-mail: editor@tourismtattler.com
Skype: tourismtattler

MAGAZINE ADVERTISING
ADVERTISING DIRECTOR Bev Langkilde
Cell: +27 (0)71 224 9971
Fax: +27 (0)86 656 3860
E-mail: bev@tourismtattler.com
Skype: bevtourismtattler

SUBSCRIPTIONS
http://eepurl.com/bocldD

BACK ISSUES (Click on the covers below)..

▼ JUL 2016	▼ JUN 2016	▼ MAY 2016

▼ APR 2016	▼ MAR 2016	▼ FEB 2016

▼ JAN 2016	▼ DEC 2015	▼ NOV 2015

▼ OCT 2015	▼ SEP2015	▼ AUG 2015

CONTENTS

EDITORIAL CONTRIBUTORS

Aadil Patel	Jarred Manasse
Adv. Louis Nel	Kim Jacobsen
Andrew Loveridge	Kirsten Caddy
Ben Coley	Martin Janse van Vuuren
David Macdonald	Paul Johnson
Dawn Burnham	Vernon Wait

MAGAZINE SPONSORS

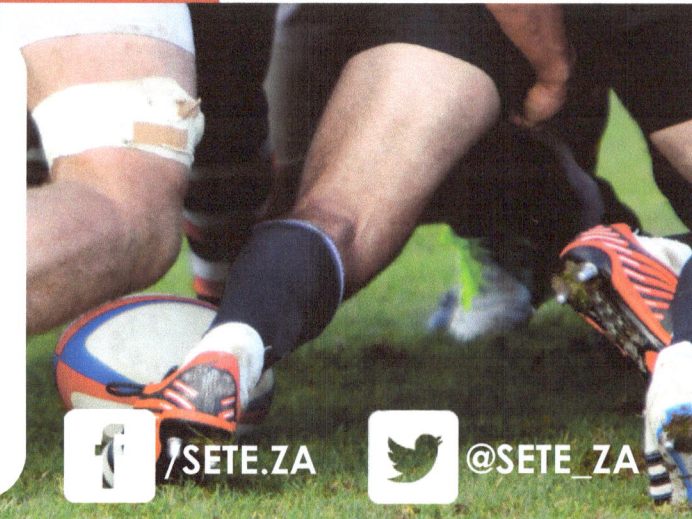

Sports & Events Tourism Exchange
CONNECT EDITION

25 - 27 October 2016
Protea Hotel Fire & Ice! Menlyn Tshwane

f /SETE.ZA   **🐦** @SETE_ZA

The 6th edition of the Sports and Events Tourism Exchange will be hosted in a CONNECT format which will give delegates equal opportunity to attend the conference sessions and schedule one-on-one meetings with international buyers and local stakeholders.

Connect /kəˈnɛkt/ – bring together or into contact so that a real link/business relationship is established.

Book your seat NOW
for R4 500.00 excl. VAT

Sports & Events Tourism Exchange Conference
This year the following themes will be focused on:

- What sponsors are looking for when supporting events;
- Technology and how it can boost your events visitor attendance/fans;
- How to measure return on investment of events;
- Travel behavior, trends and spend of golf tourists;
- Business opportunities that the 2022 Commonwealth Games could present;
- Importance of partnerships;

SPORTS & EVENTS TOURISM AWARDS
CALL FOR NOMINATIONS

The Sports & Events Tourism Awards taking place on the 26th October, is aimed at recognizing events that contribute to tourism growth, destination marketing, sports & event legacies and local economic development.

Event owners, host cities & sponsors can nominate events by submitting impact assessment reports along with supporting documentation of their events.

For more information go to www.sportsandevents.co.za/sports-and-events-tourism-awards/ or contact Cathy@ThebeReed.co.za

AWARD CATEGORIES
- ★ Best international event that contributes to tourism growth
- ★ Best domestic event that contributes to tourism growth
- ★ Best event Improving the brand profile of the destination
- ★ Best event leaving a development legacy
- ★ Best emerging township event contributing to local economic development
- ★ Best event city or province

www.sportsandevents.co.za

Organised by

Event partner

tourism
Department:
Tourism
REPUBLIC OF SOUTH AFRICA

Host City

CITY OF
TSHWANE
IGNITING EXCELLENCE

COVER STORY:

Our August edition front cover reflects the happy disposition of staff members at Lentaba Safari Lodge, located in the **Lalibela Game Reserve** in South Africa's Eastern Cape province. A fitting image considering that South Africa celebrates National Women's Day on 9 August.

On this day, 54 years ago, more than 20 000 South African women of all races staged a march on the Union Buildings in Pretoria to protest against the proposed amendments to the Urban Areas Act of 1950, commonly referred to as the "pass laws". The women stood silently for 30 minutes and then started singing a protest song that was composed in honour of the occasion: *Wathint'Abafazi Wathint'imbokodo!* (Now you have touched the women, you have struck a rock). This incarnation has since come to represent women's courage and strength in South Africa *(read more here)*.

It was not until the introduction of the Constitution of Human Rights in 1996 that all women in this country were recognized formally as equal citizens. In this Constitution, a special paragraph for women, titled 'Equality' states that you may not unfairly discriminate directly or indirectly against anyone on one or more grounds. But today South African women still have to contend with high rates of unemployment, rape and domestic violence *(read more here)*.

Although unquantified *(I'd be interested to know if any tourism academics have researched this)* the South African hospitality industry has certainly played a significant role in addressing the imbalance of employment and career advancement opportunities for women.

Like most rural enterprises, Lalibela Game Reserve by way of example, plays a vital role in the upliftment of rural women. Traditionally, rural women were restricted to menial employment opportunities, which often meant that they migrated to the cities, which in turn

lead to breaking up families as children were left behind with grandparents. Being one of the largest employers between Port Elizabeth and Grahamstown, and being able to offer career opportunities for women, means that Lalibela has played a significant role in the upliftment of rural women since it first opened in 2002.

The recent sale of Lalibela Game Reserve, which has resulted in the purchase of significant additional land, and the establishment of a new 10-bed tented camp, due to open in mid-October, will create still more opportunities for women in the surrounding rural communities *(read more on pages 26 - 29)*.

On the subject of remembrance days, in August we also celebrate World Lion Day on the 10th, and in this edition we look at the unprecedented global awareness that the death of Cecil the lion created for conservation in Africa *(read more on pages 20 - 21)*.

Keeping to the topics of hospitality and conservation, Ben Coley of Bushwise Training delves into the role of Field Guides in the business section *(read more on page 17)*.

Enjoy your read – feedback is appreciated.

Yours in Tourism,
Des Langkilde.

ACCREDITATION

Official Travel Trade Journal and Media Partner to:

The Africa Travel Association (ATA)

Tel: +1 212 447 1357 • Email: _info@africatravelassociation.org_ • Website: _www.africatravelassociation.org_

ATA is a division of the Corporate Council on Africa (CCA), and a registered non-profit trade association in the USA, with headquarters in Washington, DC and chapters around the world. ATA is dedicated to promoting travel and tourism to Africa and strengthening intra-Africa partnerships. Established in 1975, ATA provides services to both the public and private sectors of the industry.

The African Travel & Tourism Association (Atta)

Tel: +44 20 7937 4408 • Email: _info@atta.travel_ • Website: _www.atta.travel_

Members in 22 African countries and 37 worldwide use Atta to: Network and collaborate with peers in African tourism; Grow their online presence with a branded profile; Ask and answer specialist questions and give advice; and Attend key industry events.

National Accommodation Association of South Africa (NAA-SA)

Tel: +27 86 186 2272 • Fax: +2786 225 9858 • Website: _www.naa-sa.co.za_

The NAA-SA is a network of mainly smaller accommodation providers around South Africa – from B&Bs in country towns offering comfortable personal service to luxurious boutique city lodges with those extra special touches – you're sure to find a suitable place, and at the same time feel confident that your stay at an NAA-SA member's establishment will meet your requirements.

Regional Tourism Organisation of Southern Africa (RETOSA)

Tel: +27 11 315 2420/1 • Fax: +27 11 315 2422 • Website: _www.retosa.co.za_

RETOSA is a Southern African Development Community (SADC) institution responsible for tourism growth and development. RETOSA's aims are to increase tourist arrivals to the region through. RETOSA Member States are Angola, Botswana, DR Congo, Lesotho, Madagascar, Malawi, Mauritius, Mozambique, Namibia, Seychelles, South Africa, Swaziland, Tanzania, Zambia and Zimbabwe.

Southern African Vehicle Rental and Leasing Association (SAVRALA)

Contact: _manager@savrala.co.za_ • Website: _www.savrala.co.za_

Founded in the 1970's, SAVRALA is the representative voice of Southern Africa's vehicle rental, leasing and fleet management sector. Our members have a combined national footprint with more than 600 branches countrywide. SAVRALA are instrumental in steering industry standards and continuously strive to protect both their members' interests, and those of the public, and are therefore widely respected within corporate and government sectors.

Seychelles Hospitality & Tourism Association (SHTA)

Tel: +248 432 5560 • Fax: +248 422 5718 • Website: _www.shta.sc_

The Seychelles Hospitality and Tourism Association was created in 2002 when the Seychelles Hotel Association merged with the Seychelles Hotel and Guesthouse Association. SHTA's primary focus is to unite all Seychelles tourism industry stakeholders under one association in order to be better prepared to defend the interest of the industry and its sustainability as the pillar of the country's economy.

Tourism, Hotel Investment and Networking Conference 2016

Website: _www.thincafrica.hvsconferences.com_

THINC Africa 2016 takes place in Cape Town from 6-7 September.

International Coalition of Tourism Partners (ICTP)

Website: _www.tourismpartners.org_

ICTP is a travel and tourism coalition of global destinations committed to Quality Services and Green Growth.

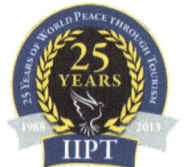

International Institute for Peace through Tourism

Website: _www.iipt.org_

IIPT is dedicated to fostering tourism initiatives that contribute to international understanding and cooperation.

World Travel Market

WTM Africa - Cape Town in April, _WTM Latin America_ - São Paulo in April, and _WTM - London_ in November. WTM is the place to do business.

The Safari Awards

Website: _www.safariawards.com_

Safari Award finalists are amongst the top 3% in Africa and the winners are unquestionably the best.

World Luxury Hotel Awards

Website: _www.luxuryhotelawards.com_

World Luxury Hotel Awards is an international company that provides award recognition to the best hotels from all over the world.

6 of the BEST NAMIBIAN SAFARI LODGES

Journeys Namibia

Images © JourneysNamibia.com

This month's **Africa Adventure Travel GeoDirectory** listing project features six of Namibia's finest safari properties, all of which are professionally managed by Journeys Namibia – a hospitality and property management company of choice for both private and community owned lodges who support sustainable eco tourism, and want their guests to have a personalised and authentic experience, which stems from service excellence by community employed personnel.

#1 Grootberg Lodge

Grootberg Lodge is perched on the rim of the Etendeka Plateau in Namibia and stands sentinel over the Klip River Valley, where 12 000 hectares have been set aside by the #Khoadi//Hoas community for conservation and tourism. Visitors can explore this pristine wilderness either by foot or car and experience encounters with the inhabitants of this remote biosphere.

Grootberg Lodge is a landmark in Namibia for the tourism industry as it is the first middle-market establishment in the country that is 100% owned by the community conservancy. For travellers making the journey between Etosha and Swakopmund, this lodge provides an ideal midway stopover, whilst allowing guests to experience the true wilderness that is Damaraland.

Read more: *View this listing here*.

#2 Hoada Campsite

Hoada Campsite is hidden among large grey granite boulders and mopani trees, in the Khoadi /Hoas conservancy 25km east of Grootberg Lodge or 75km on the C40 west from Kamanjab in Namibia.

Hoada (pronounced *Waada* - meaning "everybody") offers travellers a serene home in the wilderness. Hoada Campsite is under the same management as the Grootberg Lodge, the historic, initiative funded by the European Union and wholly owned by the people of the conservancy.

There are currently three exclusive campsites, each of which can accommodate eight people, with ample designated areas for four tents or vehicles with roof-top tents. The Group campsite can take up to 14 guests and the site has male and female ablution facilities.

Read more: *View this listing here*.

Images © JourneysNamibia.com

Journeys *Namibia*

Image © Denzel Bezuidenhout

Image © JourneysNamibia.com

#3 Hobatere Lodge

Hobatere Lodge is located 65 km north of Kamanjab on the western border of Etosha National Park. The lodge has an airstrip and is situated in a concession area of 8,808 hectares in the region of Damaraland, which is home to a wide selection of game, including elephant, lion, leopard, cheetah, giraffe, eland, and Hartmann's zebra.

The lodge can accommodate 16 guests in 6 twins, 6 doubles, and 2 single rooms. Each room has a shower, toilet and washbasin complimented with the necessary guest amenities. Each room also has a deck in front of the unit. A coffee and tea station with hot water flask (refillable at reception) is included for your convenience. The lodge has a swimming pool, restaurant, lounge, bar area, and outside veranda with views over the waterhole. A small curio shop is available.

Read more: *View this listing [here](.).*

#4 Auas Safari Lodge

Auas Safari Lodge is nestled in an expanse of African savannah in the shadow of the Auasberge Mountains - the highest mountain range in Namibia that extends for 56 kilometers, and is rich in flora and fauna. Moltkeblick (2,479 m) is the highest peak in the range, and the second highest in the country.

Auas Safari Lodge is a perfect choice for your first night in Namibia as the lodge it is located less than an hour away from the Hosea Kutako international airport near Windhoek.

The Lodge offers 16 comfortably furnished, en-suite rooms, with a terrace for guests to get in touch with the unique natural surroundings. Coffee and tea is available in each room as well as WiFi. The Lodge has a swimming pool where guests can enjoy a truly fascinating view of the sunset, game and landscape combined. Breakfast, lunch and dinner is served in the lodge dining area as well as on the patio. Bar and Lapa facilities are also available.

Read more: *View this listing [here](.).*

Journeys *Namibia*

Image © JourneysNamibia.com

#5 Fish River Lodge

If it's wide open spaces, amazing views, and an exhilarating 4x4 Namibian adventure that you're after, then Fish River Lodge is definitely for you.

Just getting to Fish River Lodge is an adventure in itself, as the 19km access road passes through river beds and across open plains edged with ragged mountains, where you may glimpse Kudu and Ostrich in the dry river beds.

Making the most of the beautiful vistas, the Fish River Lodge has been built in harmony with its stark, striking surroundings. Completed in 2009, all the buildings that make up the lodge pay tribute to the amazing landscape, offering spectacular views of the Fish River Canyon from sunrise to sunset.

Read more: *View this listing here.*

#6 Shipwreck Lodge

Launching in February 2017, Shipwreck Lodge will grace the famous Skeleton Coast Central Concession, an area covering approximately 146,600 hectares between the Hoarusib and Hoanib Rivers in the Skeleton Coast National Park, only 45 km from Möwe Bay in the Kunene Region of North-western Namibia.

This concession area is a vulnerable and irreplaceable wildlife habitat for rare and endangered species, including black rhinoceros, desert elephant, black faced impala and Hartmann's mountain zebra. Importantly it hosts the only other viable lion population in Namibia outside of the Etosha National Park. Visitors value the area for its landscapes, unique desert dwelling large mammals, traditional cultures, quality of its remoteness, sense of isolation and perception of uncrowded 'exclusivity'.

Guests can look forward to sundowners on the expansive restaurant deck or cooling off in the swimming pool, whilst appreciating the harshness of the desert.

Read more: *View this listing here.*

Image: Shipwreck of the Eduard Bohlen on Namibia's Skeleton Coast © WikiCommons

Rwanda Gorilla Safaris

African Jungle Adventures

For the ultimate nature based adventure, you can't beat a face-to-face encounter with the world's largest living primate – **gorilla**.

Gorillas are divided into two species: the eastern gorillas and the western gorillas, (*source: Wikipedia*), and all can be found in the mountainous cloud forests and lowland swamps and marshes of central Africa.

With over 14 years of experience (since 2001), **Rwanda Gorilla Safaris** – a Rwandan based tour operator and a division of **African Jungle Adventures Ltd** – specialise in gorilla trekking safaris in **Burundi**, **Congo** (DRC), **Rwanda**, and **Uganda**.

Tailor-made gorilla safaris can be combined with several other adventure activities, such as chimpanzee tracking, golden monkey tracking, wildlife safaris, photographic safaris, cultural tours, mountaineering and special interest tours.

Each once-in-a-life-time adventure is carefully planned by professional and experienced staff. Tours are guided by knowledgeable English speaking local tour guides who have an intimate understanding of the terrain, a broad knowledge on the indigenous flora and fauna, and apply international best practices in terms of safety and security protocol in each country visited.

A comfortable and well maintained fleet of 4x4 all-terrain and passenger transfer vehicles are used on all trips. The fleet includes Toyota Land Cruisers, Nissan Patrols, Land Rovers and minibuses.

Package tours ranging from 1 day excursions to 21 day extended itineraries are offered at affordable rates.

African Jungle Adventures and Rwanda Gorilla Safaris have the experience, the transport, the best guides, and the best package itineraries at the best prices. Let us take care of your clients. t

 View **Rwanda Gorilla Safaris** listing on the Africa Adventure Travel GeoDirectory HERE.

View **African Jungle Adventures** listing on the Africa Adventure Travel GeoDirectory HERE.

View the **Nuarro Lodge** listing here.

View the **Nkwichi** listing here.

View the **Ibo Island Lodge** listing here.

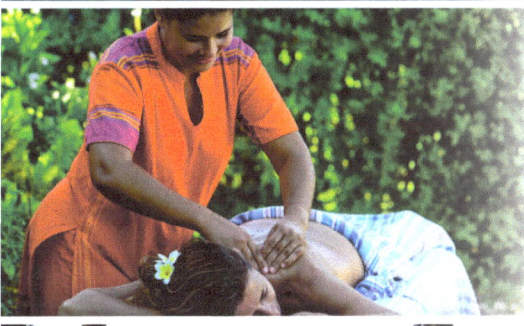

View the **Bahia Mar** listing here.

View the **Travessia Lodge** listing here.

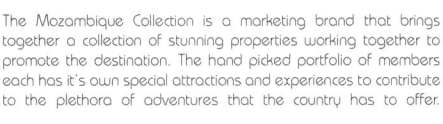

The Mozambique Collection

Small footprints, real people, exceptional experiences, amazing places …

The Mozambique Collection is a marketing brand that brings together a collection of stunning properties working together to promote the destination. The hand picked portfolio of members each has it's own special attractions and experiences to contribute to the plethora of adventures that the country has to offer.

The underlying principle of authentic luxury, in the true sense, resonates with all members – to offer the best possible experiences in idyllic locations, while creating a positive legacy for the local communities and environment in which they operate.

www.mozambique-collection.org | info@mozambioque-collection.org

Market Intelligence Report

The information below was extracted from data available as at **04 August 2016**. By **Martin Jansen van Vuuren** of **Grant Thornton**.

ARRIVALS

The latest available data from **Statistics South Africa** is for **January to May 2016***:

	Current period	Change over same period last year
UK	204 709	13.8%
Germany	133 467	20.5%
USA	131 971	18.7%
India	41 792	25.5%
China (incl Hong Kong)	49 923	59.1%
Overseas Arrivals	1 034 368	18.5%
African Arrivals	3 238 681	14.9%
Total Foreign Arrivals	4 277 673	15.7%

HOTEL STATS

The latest available data from **STR Global** is for **January** to **June 2016**:

Current period	Average Room Occupancy (ARO)	Average Room Rate (ARR)	Revenue Per Available Room (RevPAR)
All Hotels in SA	63.3%	R 1 178	R 745
All 5-star hotels in SA	65.6%	R 2 177	R 1 428
All 4-star hotels in SA	62.8%	R 1 086	R 682
All 3-star hotels in SA	62.6%	R 914	R 572
Change over same period last year			
All Hotels in SA	3.8%	8.8%	12.9%
All 5-star hotels in SA	5.6%	10.8%	16.9%
All 4-star hotels in SA	4.8%	6.5%	11.6%
All 3-star hotels in SA	3.7%	5.5%	9.4%

ACSA DATA

The latest available data from **ACSA** is for **May 2016**:

Change over same period last year	Passengers arriving on International Flights	Passengers arriving on Regional Flights	Passengers arriving on Domestic Flights
OR Tambo International	3.8%	3.0%	8.9%
Cape Town International	5.9%	26.8%	8.9%
King Shaka International	9.7%	N/A	9.8%

CAR RENTAL DATA

The latest available data from **SAVRALA** is for **January to June 2015**:

	Current period	Change over same period last year
Industry rental days	8 139 127	-1%
Industry utilisation	70.2%	-0.7%
Industry Average daily revenue	2 498 944 728	1%

WHAT THIS MEANS FOR MY BUSINESS

The data reflects the continued recovery in international arrivals. The stabilisation of the Rand in recent weeks will slow growth slightly but is not expected to have a major negative impact.

*Note that African Arrivals plus Overseas Arrivals do not add to Total Foreign Arrivals due to the exclusion of unspecified arrivals, which could not be allocated to either African or Overseas.

For more information contact Martin at Grant Thornton on +27 (0)21 417 8838 or visit: http://www.gt.co.za

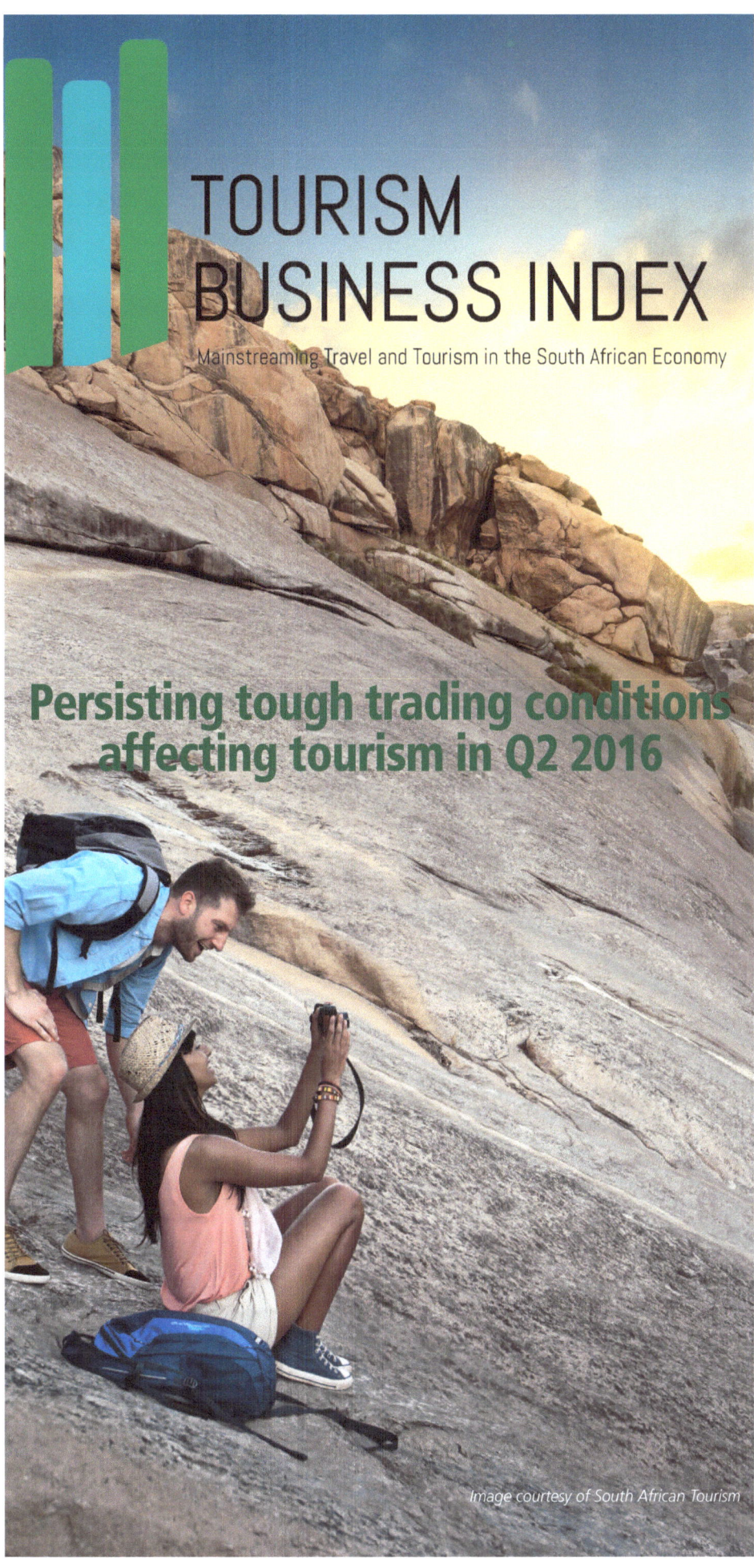

TOURISM BUSINESS INDEX

Mainstreaming Travel and Tourism in the South African Economy

Persisting tough trading conditions affecting tourism in Q2 2016

Image courtesy of South African Tourism

The Tourism Business Council of South Africa (TBCSA) reports that the persisting tough trading conditions in the South African economy are affecting businesses in the sector and have led to below normal levels of business performance as recorded in the 2016 Quarter 2 Tourism Business Index. However, the Travel and Tourism industry being the resilient sector that it is, both locally and internationally, role players have expressed hope of improved performance going forward.

These are the sentiments highlighted in the latest results of the Tourism Business Index (TBI), published by the TBCSA. The report shows that businesses in the travel and tourism sector were trading under tough conditions in Q2, recording an index score of 78.9, significantly below the score of 100 points, which indicates normal business performance levels. The score is also 7.3 index points below than the 86.2 forecasted for the second quarter of 2016.

Commenting on the outcomes of the report, TBCSA CEO, Ms. Mmatšatši Ramawela, says that the Q2 results is a clear indication that the trading environment is tougher out there hence the results that are even lower than what we were expecting in the sector following on from the impressive results of Q1. It just shows that our recovery as a sector is going to be an even bumpier ride, considering all the added pressure inherent in the broader economy, which will no doubt affect our sector. We still have the after effect of Brexit to contend with, considering that both the EU and the UK are amongst our primary source market for both our business and leisure travellers," says Ramawela.

Comparing the TBI with other economic indices in South Africa, it is apparent that there is a general trend of low confidence across South Africa's economic landscape. The Q2 2016 results of the RMB/BER Business Confidence Index fell to a score of 32, which is below the normal confidence levels (a score of 50 indicating normal). On a slightly positive note, the SACCI Business Confidence Index (BCI) showed a slight increase in the quarterly average (from 93.1 to 94.1) in Q2 2016, although the overall trend is still downward from 2015. This being the case, it is going to be critical for role players in the tourism sector to "tighten" their belts and work harder to make South Africa a compelling proposition all around.

Read More:

Download the Full TBI Q2 Report

THE BUSINESS OF FIELD GUIDING

By Ben Coley

The tourism industry is one of the most demanding industries in the world. Basically you are doing everything you can to satisfy people's expectations; people who have paid a lot of money and expect the best. For many safari goers, their first trip may well also be their last thanks to a struggling economy and inflation. In my time as a guide, an overwhelming majority of guests were visiting as part of a trip of a lifetime: a honeymoon, a 40th birthday. This is the pressure under which most tourism based establishments work: how do you make everyone's trip, a trip of a lifetime? The answers are legion: 100% commitment, courtesy, professionalism, cleanliness – the list is endless. It is not an easy job!

There are many cogs in the tourism machine, most of whom receive little to no recognition for their daily sacrifices. The next time you spend a night at a fancy establishment, spare a thought for the cleaning staff, the waiters, the scullery and the countless office-folk that made your booking possible. In the lodge industry however, one role stands head and shoulders above the rest. It is a role that has the ability to make or break a guest's stay. With hosting duties, it is not unusual for a field guide to spend as many as 16 hours a day in direct contact to your assigned guests. Those guests' experiences are therefore directly affected by the quality, enthusiasm and dedication of their guide. People come to the bush to learn about the environment and spend time among creatures that they have admired since childhood. If the food and accommodation is not up to scratch, a stay can still be rescued by a great guide.

First impressions count. This is why many lodges send their guides to meet their guests directly off the plane. They are ambassadors not only of the company in question, but also for the country. It is imperative that they look the part, their transport is clean, they are punctual and that courtesy is observed at all times. Guides work long shifts, sometimes two months or more without a day off but fatigue levels are unfortunately irrelevant. It is not the guests' fault that you are tired, you still need to give each and every visitor the same high level of service from start to finish!

Guides are a jack-of-all-trades. But one aspect trumps all others: a great guide is a people person. Sure, an in depth knowledge of the natural world is a must, but if you cannot communicate with people, the information soon becomes extraneous. A simple question: would you rather go on a game drive with a scientist who knows everything but is inaudible, rude and unmotivated; or with a newly qualified guide that has much to learn but whose enthusiasm is infectious? Facts and figures are wonderful but unless they can be quantified and moulded into an entertaining story, a guide will lose his guests' attention quickly. In my opinion, a guiding position is 70% people skills, and 30% knowledge.

A guide is on call 24 hours a day. During my time I have responded to many a guest's call during the dead of night, including being asked to remove a baby crocodile from their room (although this turned out to be a gecko!), to change lightbulbs and, as all guides are required to hold a first aid qualification, even the occasional medical complaint! It really is a job in which you give everything! But, for the right person, it is the most rewarding job in the world.

Where else can you play in the bush for ten hours a day and share those experiences with total strangers. The bush has a great way of breaking down social and economic boundaries and those brief experiences can forge friendships that last a lifetime.

A guide is an ambassador for the environment. We live in an over-populated and deteriorating world and the small areas that remain as pristine refuges for the surviving animals need to be protected. The best way to do this is by raising awareness; by infecting the general public with the need to do their part. Most visitors have zero knowledge of the intricacies of the tapestry of life and being immersed in it by a good guide can be life changing! Sure, the 'green' movement is not for everyone but if we can open the eyes of just 1% of the tourist that flock to see South Africa's great biodiversity, we have made our difference. This is job of a guide.

So, what then has the role of a guide brought to the industry in recent years? Simple: they have made the natural world understandable for the masses. People tend to fear, or at least, avoid things they do not fully understand. A guide is there to bridge that gap between the city dweller and his/her ancestry. The desire to spend time in nature is strong with all of us, but a guide is there to facilitate and resurrect that relationship; to pollinate guests with knowledge, understanding and passion. But most importantly, to do it via personal attention. That's the business of field guiding. t

About the author: Ben Coley is the head trainer at Bushwise Training. For more information: www.bushwise.co.za

The winning 'Like' or 'Share' during the month of **August 2016** will receive **1x Kalahari fragrance candle** (wild honey blend) plus **2x Glodina Luxury Hand towels** (710gsm – Storm blue colour) with the compliments of **Livingstones Supply Co –** *Suppliers of the Finest Products to the Hospitality Industry*.

'Like' / 'Share' / 'Connect' with these Social Media icons to win!

Livingston Supply Company

Tourism Tattler

Competition Rules: Only one winner will be selected each month on a random selection draw basis. The prize winner will be notified via social media. The prize will be delivered by the sponsor to the winners postal address within South Africa. Should the winner reside outside of South Africa, delivery charges may be applicable. The prize may not be exchanged for cash.

Win

Winner

Congratulations to our July 2016 Social Media winner

SIBUYA
GAME RESERVE & TENTED CAMPS
🐦 @SibuyaGameRes

Spanning the magnificent Kariega Estuary on its course to meet the warm Indian Ocean, malaria-free **Sibuya Game Reserve** is South Africa's only game reserve accessed solely by boat.

Sibuya will receive **1x Kalahari Range Bath Crystals and 1x Fragrance Candle (Khoi San)** with the compliments of **Livingstones Supply Co –** *Suppliers of the Finest Products to the Hospitality Industry.*

For more information visit www.livingstonessupplyco.com

TOURISM FOR ALL

World Tourism Day
27 September 2016

PROMOTING UNIVERSAL ACCESSIBILITY

 UNWTO

Accessible Tourism for All is about creating products and services that can be equally enjoyed by persons with disabilities, tourists and locals, families with small children, seniors and everyone else.

🔗 **wtd.unwto.org**

f **WorldTourismOrganization**

🐦 **@UNWTO**

Editors note: World Lion Day, celebrated on 10 August 2016, is an independent campaign working to highlight the importance of the lion globally and to raise lion conservation awareness worldwide. The article on page 19 is very relevant to this cause, as the death of Cecil the lion created unprecedented awareness of lion conservation in Africa. Readers may also be interested to read about the population status of lions, and many more interesting articles on lions in Edition 7 of the **SATIB Conservation Trust** newsletter, downloadable here.

Image: Cecil the lion © B. Courtenay - www.satibtrust.com

Media Coverage Analysis:
Cecil the Lion

The killing of a satellite-tagged male lion by a trophy hunter in Zimbabwe in July 2015 provoked an unprecedented media reaction. In this paper, the authors provide a chronology of events following the death of a lion nicknamed "Cecil" and analyse the global media coverage of the event spatially and temporally.

By **David W. Macdonald , Kim S. Jacobsen, Dawn Burnham, Paul J. Johnson and Andrew J. Loveridge.**

The authors of this paper recruited a media monitoring company to explore patterns in both social and editorial media globally, regionally and by country.

All peaked at the same time, so there was no evidence that any one platform was responsible for precipitating the spread of the story in advance of the others. The editorial and social media also peaked in synchrony, neither one being a forerunner or follower in the coverage of the Cecil story.

Instead, our results reveal a highly interconnected media universe: with the story going viral synchronously across media channels and geographically across the globe over the span of about two days. We consider whether the preoccupying interest in Cecil displayed by the millions of people who followed the story may betray a personal, and thus potentially political, value not just for Cecil, and not just for lions, but for wildlife, conservation and the environment. If so, then for those concerned with how wildlife is to live alongside human enterprise, this is a moment not to be squandered and one which might have the potential to herald a significant shift in society's interaction with nature.

The number of articles in the editorial media mentioning Cecil the lion peaked at 11,788 on 29 July. There was remarkable global synchrony in this "spike", so the world media appeared to respond as a globalised entity. We used media saturation, a relative measure of the number of mentions of the Cecil story, as a proxy for estimating the level of interest in the Cecil story.

Regionally, saturation levels were high in North America. Interest was also high in Australia and parts of South America and Africa. This opposes the common assumption that interest in the Cecil story was the prerogative of wealthy nations.

The social media response to Cecil's death, was much larger than that in the editorial media in terms of the number of mentions of Cecil (87,533 mentions), but the time to the peak was very similar to that of the editorial media. We compared the development of coverage of the event in the three largest social media platforms (Facebook, Twitter and YouTube) to see whether they played identifiably different roles in the development of the story through time.

Stories about Cecil the Lion in the editorial media increased from approximately 15 per day to nearly 12,000 at its peak, and mentions of Cecil the Lion in social media reached 87,533 at its peak.

We found that, while there were clear regional differences in the level of media saturation of the Cecil story, the patterns of the development of the coverage of this story were remarkably similar across the globe, and that there was no evidence of a lag between the social media and the editorial media. Further, all the main social media platforms appeared to react in synchrony. This story appears to have spread synchronously across media channels and geographically across the globe over the span of about two days.

For lion conservation in particular, and perhaps for wildlife conservation more generally, we speculate that the atmosphere may have been changed significantly.

Note: It is important to read the comment in the [Conservation Force Bulletin June 2016](#) in conjunction with the paper of Macdonald et. al. t

A Tasting note: *A fruitful collaboration with floral stylist and concept designer Alwijn Burger, better known as Blomboy, perfectly showcases the aromas of dried apricots, hints of vanilla and oak found in the Spier 21 Gables Chenin Blanc. Within the layers of flavour, white peaches, almond paste and windfall oranges contribute to the story of a complex, well-pedigreed Chenin Blanc.*

Available for purchase from *www.spier.co.za*

Turning a new leaf

Fresh beginnings on the Werf

As the ancient oaks put on a fresh coat of green leaves and the southeaster begins to blow away winter's cobwebs, it can only mean one thing: spring has arrived at Spier! It's fitting that during this season of fresh starts and new beginnings, change is stirring on the Spier Werf. After being sensitively restored, the historic farmyard became home to a bunch of new projects helping to once more make the Werf a hub of farm activity.

Eight To Go

Eight to Go has moved into the Old Kitchen overlooking the Werf.

Here you can create your own picnic from a selection of cold cuts, cheeses, salads, breads, dips and sweet treats.

Or you can pick up your pre-booked picnic before walking the dozen steps or so to the Werf's rolling lawns where you can spread out a blanket and tuck in.

Once you're done, pop in again to stock up on pantry-fillers such as olive oil, pesto, elderflower cordial, vinegars and flavoured salts.

Also be sure to stock up on Chef Decima's range of jams and preserves.

These are made with herbs, fruits and vegetables picked from the Werf's Food Garden where they're grown without using pesticides or artificial fertiliser.

The range constantly changes depending on what's in season – recent favourites include green watermelon preserve, strawberry and rose petal jam and lemon curried pickles.

*Book your basket a*t www.spierpicnics.co.za

The Farm Studio

Adjoining the historic Cow Shed on the Spier Werf is the new permanent home of the Spier Farm Studio. A hub of creativity and collaboration, the space will host artisans and artists at work on different projects throughout the year.

The studio's first residents were Heinrich Joemath and his team of five mosaicists – each graduates of the Spier Arts Academy – who recently worked here for two weeks. As part of the Danish retailer Coop's 150th birthday celebrations, its CEO Peter Høgsted commissioned Joemath to create a three-dimensional mosaic sculpture of the iconic Cirkelpigen – the much-loved logo of Coop's coffee brand, Cirkel Kaffe. The materials used included stones sourced from Spier's vineyards.

Feel at home

A night at Spier allows you to explore all that the Werf – and the rest of the farm has to offer. We're committed to keeping things fresh here too. Discover the changes we've completed at the Spier Hotel to make our farm-style rooms cosier and more comfortable than ever. *For bookings visit:* www.spier.co.za

Chef Tiaan studio

Located in the Old Cow Shed, Chef Tiaan Studio has opened with cooking stations where you can join Chef Tiaan for cooking demonstrations and classes several times a week: a fun activity for team-building, and the perfect gift for foodie friends and family. Having worked with the likes of Overture's Bertus Basson and Margot Janse of Le Quartier Francais, Chef Tiaan's relaxed and passionate approach to his food manifests itself in his gastronomic creations. He describes his style of cooking as "scatter food" – a way of making sure each forkful contains a variety of flavours.

Book your studio session here:
bookings@cheftiaan.com

SATSA CONFERENCE 2016

The 44th edition of the **Southern Africa Tourism Services Association** (SATSA) annual conference was convened at Pine Lake Inn, in White River, from 21 to 24 July 2016.

The three day event, preceded by a golf day, was a phenomenal success as evidenced by the number of social and media reports emanating from delegates in attendance.

"Encouragingly, we had a significant number of first-time SATSA Conference attendees coming through, which was in no small part due to the quality and substance of the sessions. We were fully subscribed, actually having to turn people away, and our host venue, Pine Lake Inn, as well as Greenway Woods Resort really went above and beyond to ensure delegates were well taken care of with unfaltering friendliness and service," said SATSA's CEO, David Frost.

The programme line-up addressed the most topical matters and led to robust debate and discussion by the panels and from the floor.

In his keynote address to delegates, the Minister of Tourism, Derek Hanekom provided an update on why the controversial unabridged birth certificate requirement remains in place, despite Cabinet's ruling that the regulations should be lifted over a year ago. *Read more here.*

In a session entitled, 'Planning for a sustained future', Martin Wiest, MD of Tourvest Destination Management, said companies have two options when it comes to responding to this rapidly evolving environment. He said that Businesses can either specialise, or they can invest in technology in order to compete with the disrupters in the industry. *Read more here.*

A programme session titled 'Bar vs STO

– Round 2', debated the issue of dynamic pricing and why a number of high-end safari properties have opted to move to a dynamic, and in some cases, best available rate (BAR) structure, which has created major concerns from tour operators over the many challenges this has created for them. *Read more here.*

The subject of tourist guiding was also addressed at the conference under a session titled 'Guiding – where the rubber hits the road', during which challenges around attracting and retaining talent in the tourist guiding industry was debated. Linda Pampallis, CEO of Thompsons Africa, said that the industry was struggling to make guiding an attractive career option for school and university leavers. "If we want to add five million visitors to South Africa then there aren't enough guides – we have to start 'talking up' guiding as a profession." *Read more on this debate here.*

A session on tourism transport debated 'How to make this key segment more competitive', and addressed the concerns of wheels operators, who have waited up to 18 months and longer to receive permits

for their vehicles. Jits Patel, Chief Director of the National Department of Transport, said that a new accreditation system (NTPR) would be launched on 29 July, 2016, and will be a very different process in terms of the applications and checks the department will be introducing, with the aim of creating a level playing field and removing barriers to entry. Patel said that once in place, it will take no more than 60 days from the time of application to receiving the operating licence.

Wrapping up the 44th conference, David Frost concluded by saying: "Next year, our venue choice will be governed by a number of factors, but the primary consideration will be logistics. We're hoping to grow to at least 350 people, so our decision will be largely guided by convenience and ease of access."

For information visit www.satsa.com

The table below shows where past SATSA conferences have been held. Note that from 2011 to 2013, SATSA merged its annual conference with other member associations of the Tourism Business Council of South Africa (TBCSA), under the banner of a Combined Travel & Tourism Industry Conference (SATTIC). t

PAST SATSA CONFERENCES				
Year	Dates	Location	Venue	Theme
2006	18–20 Aug	W. Cape – George	Diaz Strand Hotel	SATSA Means Business
2007	24-25 Aug	Gauteng – JNB	Indaba Hotel	Taking Tourism to the Next Level
2008	22-23 Aug	Gauteng – JNB	Grayston Hotel	Powering up Tourism
2009	21-22 Aug	W.Cape – Cape Town	Protea President	Surviving the Economic Crunch
2010	02-04 Sep	KZN – Ballito	Fairmont Zimbali	Leveraging the Big Event
2011	Merged into Combined Industry Conference (SATTIC) – event postponed			
2012	02-04 Sep	Gauteng – JNB	Protea OR Tambo	Alignment & Planning Together
2013	14-15 Oct	Gauteng – JNB	Maslow Hotel	Value of a Tourist
2014	07-09 Aug	W. Cape – Stellenbosch	Spier Hotel	New Opportunities
2015	13-15 Aug	W.Cape – George	Fancourt Hotel	Out of the fire: Working Together for Growth
2016	21-23 Jul	Mpum – White River	Pine Lake Inn	Sustainability

'Read more' article links provided courtesy of www.travelbones.co.za

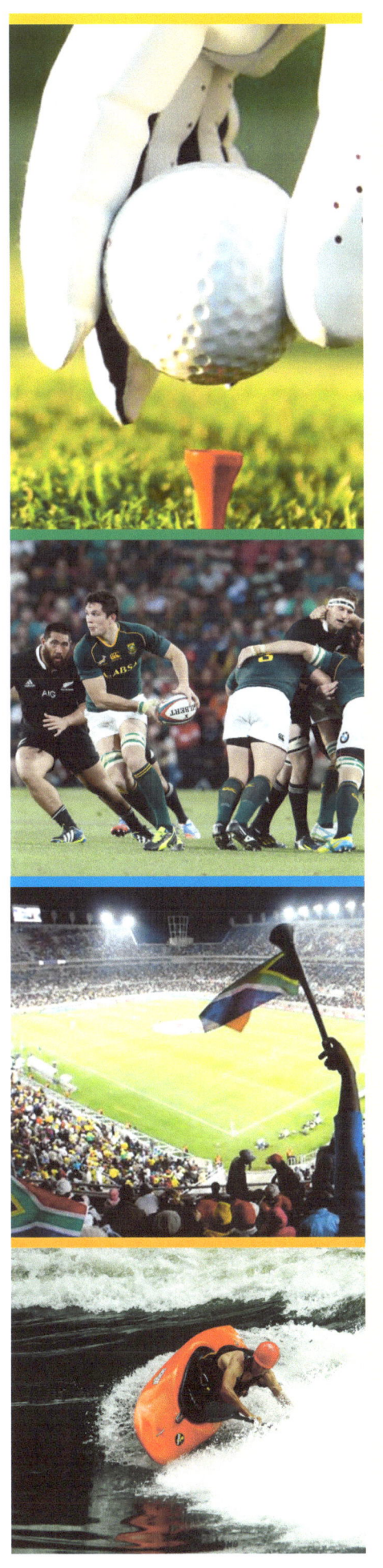

QUANTIFYING
SPORTS TOURISM

Sports Tourism is considered one of the largest and fastest-growing of all markets.

According to the United Nations World Tourism Organisation (UNWTO), sports tourism contributed $600 billion to the global travel and tourism economy in 2014.

The National Association of Sports Commissions (NASC) 2015 Report on The Sports Tourism Industry, shows that there were 25.65 million sports visitors (to the United States) in 2014, which represents a growth of 3% against 2013, while spending was estimated at $8.96 billion.

Looking at specific sports tourism segments, the 2015 Rugby World Cup saw record demand for tickets and an estimated extra 466,000 overseas visitors arriving in Britain during the tournament. VisitBritain's research recorded a record-breaking 12 per cent rise in the number of inbound visitors for October 2015, compared with the same month the year before.

In South Africa, Golf Tourism statistics collated by Sports Marketing Surveys of SA, estimate that the South African golf industry generated a total revenue of 29.2 billion ZAR and created over 50 000 jobs. The overall worth of the golf industry, including the multiplier effect, is estimated to be R58.4 billion, not to mention the foreign investment in the myriad of Golf Estates on the African continent.

Following the successful hosting of the 2010 FIFA World Cup there has been a growing interest in sports tourism in South Africa. More than 10% of foreign tourists come to South Africa to watch or participate in sport events, with spectators accounting for 60% to 80% of these arrivals.

Sports Tourism Classification*

There are several classifications on sport tourism, which can be defined as Hard Sports Tourism and Soft Sports Tourism.

Hard Sports Tourism refers to the quantity of people participating at a competitive sport events. Normally these kinds of events are the motivation that attract visitors visits the events. Olympic Games, FIFA World Cup, F1 Grand Prix and regional events such as NASCAR Sprint Cup Series could be described as hard sports tourism.

Soft Sports Tourism is when the tourist travels to participate in recreational sporting, or signing up for leisure interests. Hiking, Skiing and Canoeing can be described as soft sports tourism. Perhaps the most common form of soft sports tourism involves golf. A large number of people are interested in playing some of the world's greatest and highest ranked courses, and take great pride in checking those destinations off of their list of places to visit.

Sports Tourism can be further classified into three types:

- **Sport events tourism**: refers to the visitors who visit a city to watch events. The two events that attract the most tourist worldwide are the Olympics and the FIFA World Cup.

- **Celebrity and nostalgia sport tourism**: involves visits to the sports halls of fame and venue and meeting sports personalities in a vacation basis.

- **Active sport tourism**: refers to those who participate in the sports or events.

Source: Wikipedia

SETE 2016, South Africa

From a South African perspective, the annual Sports and Events Tourism Exchange (SETE) is the only event of its kind in Africa, and provides a platform that brings together businesses from the Sports, Events & Tourism industries, and encourages collaboration between these sectors, consisting of a two day conference, table top exhibition and networking events.

The 6th Edition of SETE will be convened at the Protea Hotel Fire & Ice in Tshwane, Gauteng from 25 to 27 October 2016, and will be hosted in a CONNECT format – dedicated to maximising delegates networking and one-on-one meeting opportunities. *Read more here*.

For more info visit www.thebereed.co.za

A New Era for Private Sector Conservation in Eastern Cape:

LALIBELA GAME RESERVE

By **Vernon Wait**

The recent sale of Lalibela Game Reserve, together with substantial parcels of land adjacent to Lalibela, is seen as a major vote of confidence in South Africa's Eastern Cape game lodge industry as a whole.

Land Acquisition

Not only is the malaria-free "Big-5 area" of Lalibela increasing in size, but the acquisition of an additional 2,000 hectares adjacent to the existing Big-5 area, means that Lalibela now has a pristine wilderness range that will be used as a breeding area, and to reintroduce endemic game species to the Eastern Cape, thus ensuring long term sustainability of game numbers.

Regarding Lalibela's flora and fauna, a huge amount of the initial effort and resources are being allocated to eradicate alien vegetation. With the addition of more land, there is a need to get game numbers up to equilibrium in terms of an ideal carrying capacity. To this end, various species of game are being acquired and these are being introduced both in the "Big-5 area" as well as in the new breeding area.

Responsible Tourism

The new owners of Lalibela are avid conservationists who acquired Lalibela because of their two passions – the preservation of African flora and fauna and the upliftment of rural communities, specifically children in rural communities.

For the conservation of habitat and wildlife to be successful over the long term, there has to be "buy-in" from local, rural communities – Africa has a long list of successful examples of this. A strong ethos at Lalibela is that the mere creation of rural jobs does not constitute rural upliftment. Going forward, Lalibela will play an active role in the meaningful upliftment of the rural communities near Lalibela.

SOUTH AFRICA - EASTERN CAPE

GPS: 33° 28′ 14.081″ S / 26° 15′ 8.733″ E

LALIBELA GAME RESERVE

The goals of conservation and community upliftment can only be sustainable over the long term if they are matched by tourism offerings that are run on sound commercial principles.

Product Refinement & Expansion

So, whilst much effort is being spent on the flora and fauna side, Lalibela recognises that the lodge and game experience that Lalibela provides for guests, needs to be consistantly at a level to ensure that support from the travel trade continues, and that it grows.

To this end Lalibela will be broadening it's offering by adding a new 10-bed tented camp, due to open in mid-October. Whilst the idea is to add additional capacity by way of extra rooms at existing lodges as well as a private villa, these ideas will be communicated to the travel trade only once they become firm plans.

Partnering with the Travel Trade

There is much debate about the role of the tour operator and travel agent in these times of rapid technological change. Lalibela believes that the travel trade has a significant role to play in the lodge industry, given the complexities of seasonality, logistics, and the like that come into play when deciding on the safari portion of an itinerary – knowledge that only a travel professional can provide.

With all the exciting changes taking place at Lalibela, this is the ideal time for travel trade professionals to contact Lalibela Game Reserve and to learn about the various developments taking place.

For more info contact Vernon on +27 (0)41 581 8170 or email *bookings@lalibela.co.za* or visit *www.lalibela.net*

*About the Author: Vernon Wait is the Managing Director of **Pembury Tours** - a leading SATSA accredited tour operator established in 1996, and offering tour itineraries across Southern and Eastern Africa.*
For more info visit www.pemburytours.com

"The only man I envy is the man who has not yet been to Africa – for he has so much to look forward to"

MOZAMBIQUE

View the Ibo Island Lodge activity video at:
Africa Adventure Travel GeoDirectory

IBO ISLAND LODGE

The award nominated and unique **Ibo Island Lodge** is the only luxury lodge on the island, and has been described as one of the most magical lodges in Africa. Located on a prime waterfront site, the lodge encompasses magnificent mansions each over one hundred years old with walls over a meter thick and lofty ceilings.

Ibo Island, or as the locals call it: *Ilha do Ibo* is situated on the Indian Ocean just 71 nm from mainland Pemba City, northern Mozambique. This island is the perfect place to explore the beaches and beauty of the Quirimbas Archipelago and National Park in Northern Mozambique. Nominated for World Heritage status, Ibo is remote and still relatively untouched by commercial development.

Accommodation

Some rooms are sea facing, and some are garden facing. All rooms are individually designed and unique. The wide verandas are furnished with hand crafted furniture and soft cushions. All rooms are air- conditioned and also have ceiling fans. The lodge has two swimming pools set in tropical gardens, an air-conditioned lounge, and private dining room.

Restaurant

The restaurant and bar is situated on the roof terrace of the Bela Vista mansion facing west for spectacular views and unforgettable sunsets over the bay. Cuisine combines Mozambican and world inspired influences with surf-fresh seafood platters, smoked sail fish, coconut and chilli traditional Ibo Island crab curry, crunchy green pawpaw, ginger prawn salad, and everyone's classical favourite creamy lobster thermidor being just some of the highlights on the menu.

Activities

Guests partake in a multitude of experiences: beach, sail, swim or fish. Special activities enable guests to immerse themselves in the unchanged, ancient culture of Ibo and the rare chance to interact with the wonderfully hospitable islanders.

Island hopping Dhow Safaris

Ibo Island Lodge is the <u>only</u> operator to offer fully guided tailor-made and scheduled departure island hopping dhow and kayak safaris. Under the expert leadership of a guide and local crew, explore the coastline or venture up river mouths teeming with red listed bird species and some of the largest mangrove forests in Africa. Snorkel off deserted white sandbanks and into turquoise sea, and sleep in mobile eco fly camps on uninhabited tropical islands. The crew conjures up fresh seafood and traditional cuisine over an open fire under island stars, leaving you free to soak up a once in a lifetime Mozambique safari.

Lastly, but perhaps more importantly Ibo Island Lodge was built with the community, and today either directly or indirectly benefits a large part of Ibo's population. Here your visit really does make a difference.

For more info visit www.iboisland.com

- The Mozambique Collection -

Ibo Island Lodge is a proud member of The Mozambique Collection - a showcase of the most exciting, unique and intimate destinations, accentuating the variety found in Mozambique, one of Africa's most incomparable, rapidly developing and beautiful countries.

The brand brings together a collection of stunning properties working together to promote the destination. The hand picked portfolio of members each has it's own special attractions and experiences to contribute to the plethora of adventures that the country has to offer.

The underlying principle of authentic luxury, in the true sense, resonates with all members – to offer the best possible experiences in idyllic locations, while creating a positive legacy for the local communities and environment in which they operate.

For more information visit www.mozambique-collection.org

Large scale
RETRENCHMENTS
different routes for different challenges

By **Kirsten Caddy** and **Aadil Patel**.

Section 189A of the Labour Relations Act, No 66 of 1995 (LRA) enumerates the rules applicable in large scale retrenchments.

Employees who are retrenched in terms of a retrenchment process pursuant to s189A have the right to challenge both the substantive and procedural fairness of their dismissals. They can do so through adjudication or strike action. South Africa has seen a limited number of strikes as a result of retrenchments.

Section 189A provides for a bifurcated process in terms of which separate remedies are created to challenge substantive fairness and procedural fairness. Where the procedural fairness of a mass retrenchment is challenged, it is necessary for the employees to bring an application (motion proceedings) to the Labour Court in terms of s189A(13). Action proceedings are not permitted to deal with procedural challenges.

However, when a dismissal is alleged to be substantively unfair, employees may choose to further their interests by resorting to strike action, alternatively, by referring a dispute to the Labour Court for adjudication. If employees elect to challenge their dismissals by referring a dispute to the Labour Court regarding whether there was a fair reason for their dismissals, such employees are precluded from embarking on strike action in respect of that dispute.

The intention of s189A of the LRA is to exclude procedural issues from the determination of substantive fairness where the employees have opted for adjudication rather than industrial action, providing instead for a mechanism to pre-empt procedural problems before the substantive issues become ripe for adjudication or industrial action.

In the recent decision in SACCAWU and P Dzivhani and 12 others v Southern Sun Hotel Interests (Pty) Ltd, the employees elected to refer a dispute to the Labour Court (as opposed to embarking on strike action) in order to challenge the substantive fairness of their dismissal. They had also brought an application to challenge the procedural fairness of the retrenchment process. The employees then applied to consolidate the referral (challenging substantive fairness) and the application (challenging procedural fairness) in order for the two issues to be heard simultaneously.

The court found that the consolidation or any other co-hearing of the procedural and substantive challenges raised in large scale retrenchments is impermissible in terms of the LRA.

While consolidation of connected claims is provided for in the Labour Court Rules, where a statute prevents consolidation, it is unnecessary to even decide whether the conditions under the rules for consolidation apply or not. Accordingly, the court found that it lacked the jurisdiction to order consolidation even if it was convenient to do so and would not prejudice the employer.

Employees are therefore obliged to pursue separate procedures in order to challenge the substantive fairness of their dismissals on the one hand and the procedural fairness of their dismissals on the other.

In addition to that, when challenging the substantive fairness of their dismissals, employees are provided with an election between embarking on industrial action and referring a dispute to the Labour Court for adjudication.

When employees make an election to refer a substantive fairness dispute to adjudication before the Labour Court, they may not embark on strike action in relation to that substantive fairness dispute. t

Published with acknowledgment to Cliffe Dekker Hofmeyr Attorneys.

This series of articles explores the legal aspects associated with the risks of operating an adventure tourism business, with specific relevance to the legal framework applicable to South Africa. Part 1 can be found on page 25 of the June 2016 edition or read the article online here.

Part 2

By 'Louis The Lawyer'

Image courtesy of Canopy Tours

ADVENTURE TOURISM
from a legal perspective

Clearly the topic gives rise to many issues as the word *'adventure'* implies a definite element of risk and with it issues such liability, responsibility, accountability and insurance. Furthermore the fact that many of the activities listed in the previous article take place in natural environments means the impact thereof on nature and surrounds need to be addressed – the latter is not only about the participant footprint but also the difficulty of access in the case of an emergency and communications.

Let's consider the issue of risk and deal with it in the sequence that participation will unfold:

NATIONALITY OF PARTICIPANT ('Pax')

- Each country has different laws and approaches to risk e.g. in Europe indemnities are frowned upon (Article on recent EC directive to follow soon)
- It is therefore imperative that the service provider ('SP') provides in its terms and conditions ('T&C') that South African law & jurisdiction will apply
- The impact of the aforementioned can be ameliorated further by the inclusion in the T&C of comprehensive mediation and arbitration clause – this not only is a great plus as far as brand management is concerned but is also less expensive and quicker.

SERVICE PROVIDERS ('SP')

- Each case may well be different i.e. it may be the pax 'doing his own thing' ('FIT') thus booking the entire trip from/back to country of origin and participating without a guide/professional assistance; conversely it may involve the pax, a travel agent, tour operator and a guide or a combination of the aforesaid.
- The important aspect here from a legal perspective is the network of contracts and 'cross-indemnities' involved – between each of the parties mentioned in the preceding paragraph there should be clearly demarcated risk (profile and acceptance) and with it liability, responsibility, accountability and insurance and this should be contained in a written, signed contract.

BOOKING

- The booking can be online and/or involving one or more of the SP mentioned above – it is advisable to ensure clear acceptance of risk and an audit trail. It may seem 'airy fairy' until an actual claim arises!
- As the Consumer Protection Act, Act 68 of 2008 ('the CPA') will play a material role in the risk scenario, liability and the indemnity, strict adherence is required to sections pertaining to such as non-refundable deposits/cancellation (17), disclosure/transparency (41 & 49), liability (48, 51 & 61) and the content of the terms per se (Regulation 45) (See discussion in next insert).
- Cognizance will also have to be taken of the information disclosed by the Pax and managed by the SP in terms of the Protection of Personal Information Act, Act 4 of 2013 ('the POPI') – given the no fault liability approach contained in POPI, insurance is imperative.

TERMS AND CONDITIONS ('T&C')

I have from time to time been asked why there is a need for T&C (1) by a travel agent who was under the false impression that it was protected by the supplier/tour operator's T&C; (2) When there is an indemnity!

Both questions of course are of a serious nature especially when the 1st comes from 'an old hand' in tourism and the 2nd from an experienced underwriter!

The answer to the 1st question is that unless very specifically drafted/worded, the supplier/tour operator's T&C will not extend to/protect the travel agent

The answer to the 2nd question is that unless very specifically drafted/worded, the indemnity does not usually deal with issues such as limitation of liability, law and jurisdiction, domicilium, interest in late payments, passports and visa, health risks etc – this is usually the domain of the T&C so you need both (T&C & indemnity).

To be continued.

Looking to CHINA for SA INBOUND Tourists

By **Enver Duminy**, CEO, Cape Town Tourism.

Billions of rands are being invested into South Africa by Chinese corporations, trade delegations are coming and going on official visits, and interest in South Africa is on the rise in terms of tourism. SA Tourism recently convened four workshops attended by Cape Town Tourism across China in order for SA suppliers to showcase their products and update the Chinese market on new offerings.

These workshops involved 420 agents, and provided significant networking opportunities, allowing for the creation and consolidation of new business and trade as well as boosting confidence in SA among outbound operators and travel agents.

Key market insights

According to "The Future of Chinese Travel" report, South Africa is amongst the top 15 destinations for Chinese tourists with Gauteng being the second most popular city in the MEA region for Chinese travellers. South Africa is also amongst the top 15 destinations in terms of the Chinese share of total travel spending, which is expected to grow from US$0.5 billion in 2013 to more than US$3 billion in 2023.

In South Africa, the Chinese outbound tourism arrival has reached 84 878 in 2015, increased by 2.2% YOY. If it wasn't for the visa regulation plunge, it would be much higher.

Chinese community and investments

The distance from China to South Africa is approximately 12,000km, which means it take at least 15 hours to travel between the two countries by plane. Despite the distance, Chinese restaurants, China Malls, and Chinatowns are everywhere in South Africa. Research conducted in 2010 shows there are over 500,000 Chinese people in this country, according to Dr Yoon Jung Park, the coordinator of the Chinese in Africa/ Africans in China International Research Working Group at Rhodes University.

China is now South Africa's largest trading partner both in exports and imports, with trade between the two countries over R100 billion. By the end of 2015, South Africa and China had signed 26 agreements worth R94 billion.

Since the workshops took place in different cities across China, disparate preferences were discovered. Visitors from Beijing have different expectations from those in Xi'an.

Beijing:

Beijing is considered a tier-one market city as there is general awareness of SA: 40% of agents in Beijing are new to selling SA and Cape Town as a destination, but agents have been exploring the country on personal visits which have allowed for some exposure. They have returned to China with positive reports.

They are most likely to come on package tours, and know about Tsogo Sun & Sun International, travelling by Air China and Cathay Pacific. Typical travel schedules are from Johannesburg to Kruger and Sun City to Cape Town. They stay 10 days in SA, 4 of

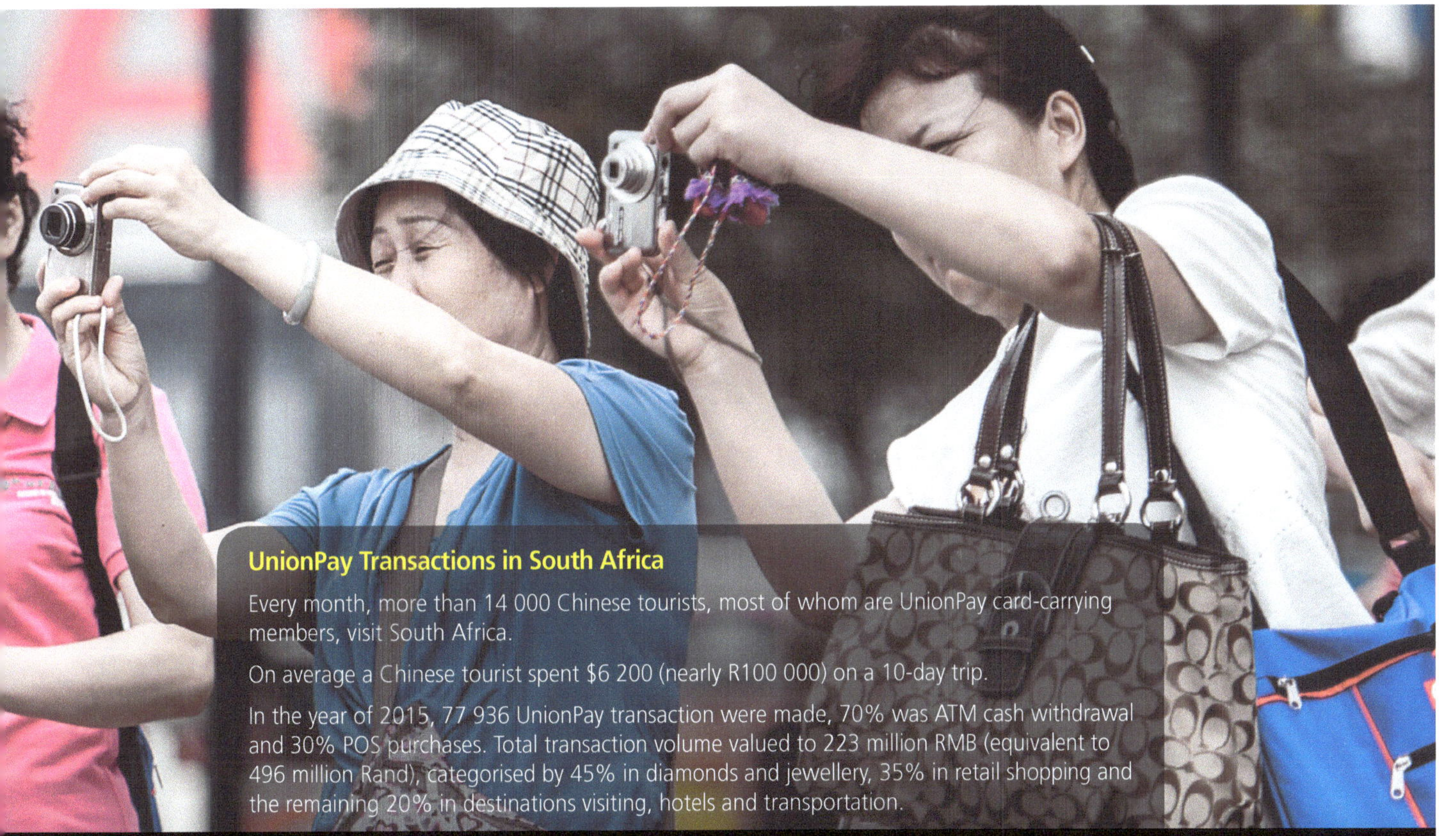

UnionPay Transactions in South Africa

Every month, more than 14 000 Chinese tourists, most of whom are UnionPay card-carrying members, visit South Africa.

On average a Chinese tourist spent $6 200 (nearly R100 000) on a 10-day trip.

In the year of 2015, 77 936 UnionPay transaction were made, 70% was ATM cash withdrawal and 30% POS purchases. Total transaction volume valued to 223 million RMB (equivalent to 496 million Rand), categorised by 45% in diamonds and jewellery, 35% in retail shopping and the remaining 20% in destinations visiting, hotels and transportation.

which are spent in Cape Town (for leisure travellers in particular). Top months are Jan – Feb (the Chinese New Year) and May – June (annual holidays).

Beijing business travellers travel any time of year with fewer restrictions, enjoying golf, wine and cultural experiences.

Guangzhou:

Also a tier-one city, Guangzhou enjoy luxury travel, including visits to top restaurants like the Test Kitchen, retail experiences and visits to top attractions such as Table Mountain and Cape Point. They are typically corporate visitors who come to Cape Town in July and stay for five days. They are considered high-end consumers. The majority of agents in Guangzhou use SAA and Qatar Airlines.

Xi'an:

As a tier-two city, agents in Xi'an needed more awareness made of SA's products and attractions, however, this is a high end consumer market base not interested in packaged tours.

Interest was expressed in the following angles: Westernised gourmet food, local and domestic flights – private jets if possible, adventure experiences such as abseiling, hiking and whale tours and a huge interest in Cape Town's Jazz Festival, Carnival, Fashion Week and Marathon.

Preferred airlines include Air China via Hong Kong and an air access opportunity would be via Kenya Airways - fly direct to CPT – Kenya.

Hangzhou:

Hangzhou is another smaller city that is getting to know South Africa and Cape Town. Quite a few agents have visited, and visitors

from that city are high-end consumers, but more likely to book as groups rather than as individuals. They expressed an interest in self-drive tours from Cape Town into the Western Cape, and would like to take part in adventure activities such as snorkeling with seals, paragliding from Table Mountain and bicycle tours. As with the other cities, Hangzhou visitors would like to see the Big 7: Robben Island Museum, Kirstenbosch, the City Walk, Cape Point, Groot Constantia, Table Mountain Cableway and specifically V&A Waterfront.

Local businesses that are already active within the Chinese Market that attended the workshops included luxury hotel groups and tour companies, while other key players included exclusive jewelers such as Shimansky and First Diamonds and attractions such as Cape Point and V&A Waterfront, both of which maintain a presence in China.

As with any potential market, the key is to keep the destination at top of mind for agents.

Adding value through consistent introduction of new products and reinvention of older ones will ensure that there's always something fresh on offer to visitors.

For more info visit: www.capetown.travel

Cape Town based travel company Drive South Africa has partnered with Google through the Google Street View camera loan program to capture 360-degree street view imagery of South Africa's top wilderness, cultural and historic sites for Google Maps.

By **Jarred Manasse**

Each "off-road" location will be captured with Google's Street View Trekker, a wearable backpack topped with a camera system designed by Google. The Street View Trekker backpack is walked through trails or pedestrian walkways on foot, and automatically gathers images as it goes.

Google Street View gives internet users a virtual tour of an area using 360-degree panoramic photographs.

South Africa's roads were added to Google Street View in 2010 ahead of the FIFA World Cup.

The first phase of the project has seen 22 volunteer trekkers cover 33 trails across the Cape Peninsula, including seven routes up Table Mountain, five beaches and three urban trails such as the Sea Point promenade.

The team has explored more than 150 kilometres on foot over a six week period and will cover nature reserves across the country over the next few months.

The project has gained support from various tourism stakeholders: Wesgro - the official tourism, trade and investment promotion agency for Cape Town and the Western Cape, SANParks, Cape Nature, Ezemvelo KZN Wildlife and lead project partner South African Tourism.

"We are very excited to back this opportunity to deliver the real South Africa to people all over the world via Google's widely used platforms," said Margie Whitehouse, Chief Marketing Officer of SA Tourism.

The project comes in the wake of Google's launch of South Africa: Mzansi Experience in March 2016, which helped the world explore South Africa's iconic destinations such as the Kruger National Park, Table Mountain, and the Cape of Good Hope via 360-degree imagery from the comfort of the viewers armchair. t

About the author: Jarred Manasse is the Content Manager at Drive South Africa. For more information: www.drivesouthafrica.co.za

MAPPING South Africa's Trails

Help trek South Africa's trails

Andre Van Kets, co-founder of Drive South Africa, is heading up the #TrekSouthAfrica campaign. Van Kets hopes to get locals from across the country to assist in mapping out Mzansi's trails and tourist attractions.

"We have an epic six-month trip planned, with over 20 national parks, eight UNESCO World and many other wonderful destinations in all nine provinces on our schedule." said Van Kets.

"We want to engage with individuals and local communities along the way, so that we can bring Mzansi's best attractions to Google Street View. We're looking for people to suggest highlights in their areas, help us trek their neck of the woods and ultimately be a part of this exciting project. We want this to be a campaign by South Africans from all walks of life."

To learn more or apply to volunteer as a local trekker visit the #TrekSouthAfrica website.

Tourism Tattler is onboard. Will you be?

▲ Volunteer trekker Ivan Breetzke joined the #TrekSouthAfrica team for a hike in Kirstenbosch Botanical Gardens in June 2016. Photo: Andre Van Kets.

▲ Behind the scenes: #TrekSouthAfrica project lead Andre Van Kets helps Devon Krantz load-up the 22kg Google Trekker backpack as Carte Blanche cameraman Greg Nelson captures the moment with Hout Bay in the background, June 2016. Photo: Liz Fish.

▼ 26 Volunteer trekkers and two dogs joined for a trek up Noordhoek Peak in the Table Mountain National Park in June 2016, part of the #TrekSouthAfrica project. Photo: Rudolph De Girardier.

Ford Mustang

By Steve Conradie

There is nothing that sounds quite like the grunt of Mustang's 5.0L V8. Although the models have changed over the years that sound has remained a hallmark. It's probably not as loud as it's predecessors but Ford has ensured that the new 2015 Mustang remains the icon it has been for more than 50 years.

The new factory made right hand drive is a welcome sight for the South African market and in my opinion is priced to do well. The fact that Ford's order book is already full for the foreseeable future is telling of it's popularity and path to success.

At first glance the Mustang turns heads. And to my surprise a lot of heads! It did not help that the demo model I had the pleasure of test driving was a bright Triple yellow.

Ford has done well to modernise the legendary design without compromising on the Mustang's classic and distinctive looks, retaining that aggressive grill with the iconic galloping horse, nostalgic sport back and fin like tail lights.

The interior is modern and boasts the latest Sync2 touchscreen display yet has a subtle underlying retro style that compliments the Mustang brand well. It feels a bit like the cockpit of a fighter jet with push button start, chrome toggle switches and bright electronic instrument clusters. The handbrake, however is positioned on the left hand side of the center console and is awkward to operate. It's as if they forgot to move it to the right when they decided to introduce right hand drive.

There is a host of performance features that will wow any enthusiast. Using the latest Selective Drive Modes you can choose from various steering options, change performance settings (there is a handy engine performance indicator in track mode), set launch control (manual only), and many other mind blowing settings that will thrill any level of driver. These are backed by equally impressive safety features such as ABS, tyre pressure monitoring, strategically positioned airbags, electronic stability control, body design that improves road handling and the list goes on.

What surprised me the most is how spacious the car is in general. Being all of 184cm I felt very comfortable sitting in the driver's seat with outstretched legs and headroom to spare. The rear seats are bigger than what you would find in similar sportback although it still won't fit the average adult comfortably but there is plenty of space for kids. I was able to fit a baby seat in the back. It may not quite be the image a die hard Mustang owner would want to portray but the point I was trying to make is that the Mustang can very well be an everyday car. The boot is large at 384L and I was able to fit my golf clubs with ease.

The best part is the drive. Mustang has the power and performance to match that awesome sound. The acceleration is just exhilarating! The handling is unbelievable yet feels extremely safe. The new independent suspension and direct drive to the rear axle hugs the road with ease. The drive is pure pleasure!

The mighty 5.0L V8 is pure grunt at 303kw and 525Nm. It has no turbo yet achieves an impressive 4.8sec for 0-100kph. My fuel consumption for the test was around 14L/100km, a little higher than the rated average of 12L/100km. That included a combination of urban and rural driving with a little heavy footed accelerations on a few occasions - which one does when testing a V8 GT!

The 5.0L GT is marked at R839 900 for the automatic fastback and R899 900 for the convertible

There is the cheaper 2.3L turbocharged Ecoburst version which produces 233kw and 432Nm priced at R719 211 for the auto fastback and R779 900 for the convertible, but I don't know why anyone would buy one. It's that thrilling V8 that makes the GT the model to buy! All models include a 4 year / 120 000km comprehensive warranty and 5 year / 100 000km service plan with 20 000km intervals. [t]

About the author: Tattler correspondent Steve Conradie is a seasoned vehicle reviewer and Director at Drive South Africa www.drivesouthafrica.co.za

www.ingramcontent.com/pod-product-compliance
Lightning Source LLC
Chambersburg PA
CBHW050401180526
45159CB00005B/2110